Brav
Little M

Once upon
a time, a lion,
a tiger, and a mouse
lived in a forest.
One night, the animals
all heard a terrible noise.
Ooooo! Ooooo! Ooooo!
They were VERY frightened.

The next morning,
Lion and Tiger said,
"We are big and strong.
We will find the monster
that is making that noise
and make it go away."

So away they went,
SWISHING through the grass,
JUMPING over boulders,
SLOPPING through the mud,
PANTING up the mountain.

They came to a cave,
but, just as they looked inside,
they heard the terrible noise.
Ooooo! Ooooo! Ooooo!

Lion and Tiger were so
frightened that they ran back
home as fast as they could.

In the morning,
Mouse said, "I'm going
to find the monster."

"YOU?" roared Lion
and Tiger. "YOU? Why,
you're not big and strong
like us!" Lion and Tiger
laughed and laughed.

But away Mouse went, SWISHING through the grass, JUMPING over boulders, SLOPPING through the mud, PANTING up the mountain.

She came to the cave.
Then she heard the noise.
Ooooo! Ooooo! Ooooo!

Mouse was frightened,
but she went into the cave.
She saw that it wasn't
a monster at all!
It was the wind
whistling through
a hole
in the cave.

The noise stopped.
Mouse saw that a big rock
had fallen over the hole.
Then she quickly ran home.

"I found the monster
and stopped the noise,"
she said. "Mice are not big,
but they are clever and brave!"
No one laughed at Mouse again.